KING CAT

Written by Swapna Haddow

Illustrated by Max Rambaldi

King Cat wasn't a great king. In fact, he wasn't even a good king.

He was a terrible king ...

... because he was a *cat*.

And he wasn't even a great cat at that, because the palace mice clearly had the run of the castle.

You see, when the queen died with no heir to the throne, she left a will telling everyone who should be in charge:

If I die, King Cat must sit upon the throne.

The queen also left many, many, many more instructions.

She commanded that her beloved cat should eat only the finest and freshest salmon from the lake …

… and that her cherished cat must drink milk only from a golden chalice …

… and that her much-loved cat must have six hundred and forty-three naps a day …

… and that all the door handles in the kingdom should be lowered to her darling cat's height, so he could go wherever he pleased.

This sounded rather strange to the people of the kingdom, but they trusted their dear queen and loyally followed her wishes.

On the day of King Cat's coronation, he refused to follow the coronation route and instead created his own. He strutted over the window ledges of nearby buildings, making it very tricky for the coronation carriages to follow.

He then used the crown as his litter tray, much to the royal jeweller's dismay.

He also refused to sit still for the official royal painting — and decided to paint the official royal painter, instead.

"I cannot work in these conditions!"

The peasantry started to despair. With no-one but a cat in power to rule the kingdom, food and water began to run low.

The royal adviser knew something had to be done.

Late one night, whilst looking for a solution, she found a golden scroll.

Here was something that could solve all of the kingdom's problems!

She kept the parchment safe, and sent out the royal postal pigeon with an important letter.

The letter arrived at the door of a young man. He read the letter, gasped, and left for the palace immediately.

When he arrived, the royal adviser was very pleased to see him. She took him straight to the royal court.

"This man has a rightful claim as a successor to the throne," she announced.

"He is the late queen's great aunt's cousin's niece's brother's aunt's uncle's daughter's nephew's son!"

The court was alive with excitement, as they waited to see if King Cat would do something …

… but he was having his five hundred and ninety-third nap of the day, so it fell upon the people to decide what should happen to the monarchy.

"The queen's wishes were clear," a member of the court said. "Only King Cat must sit upon the throne."

The adviser smiled, and then asked the stranger to tell the court his name.

"Catan," the man replied.

The court gasped.

"Sir," the adviser said excitedly, "all you must do is shorten your name to Cat. Then the queen's wishes will be upheld, and you can sit upon the throne — and rule as the new king! You are part of the royal family, after all."

And so, the new King Cat took the throne, with sceptre and orb in hand, and vowed to reign graciously for as long as he lived.

Well, actually King Cat sat on a chair next to the throne, where the queen's cat continued to have his naps.

And he had only the sceptre, because the cat had grown rather fond of the orb.

Published by Pearson Education Limited, 80 Strand, London, WC2R 0RL.

www.pearsonschools.co.uk

Text © Pearson Education Limited 2020

Written by Swapna Haddow

Project managed and edited by Just Content Limited

Original illustrations © Pearson Education Limited 2020

Illustrated by Max Rambaldi

Designed and typeset by Collaborate Agency Limited

This publication is protected by copyright, and permission should be obtained from the publisher prior to any prohibited reproduction, storage in a retrieval system, or transmission in any form or by any means, electronic, mechanical, photocopying, recording, or otherwise. For information regarding permissions, request forms and the appropriate contacts, please visit https://www.pearson.com/us/contact-us/permissions.html Pearson Education Limited Rights and Permissions Department.

Unless otherwise indicated herein, any third party trademarks that may appear in this work are the property of their respective owners and any references to third party trademarks, logos or other trade dress are for demonstrative or descriptive purposes only. Such references are not intended to imply any sponsorship, endorsement, authorisation, or promotion of Pearson Education Limited products by the owners of such marks, or any relationship between the owner and Pearson Education Limited or its affiliates, authors, licensees or distributors.

First published 2020

23 22 21 20

10 9 8 7 6 5 4 3 2 1

British Library Cataloguing in Publication Data

A catalogue record for this book is available from the British Library

ISBN 978 0 435 20165 4

Copyright notice

All rights reserved. No part of this publication may be reproduced in any form or by any means (including photocopying or storing it in any medium by electronic means and whether or not transiently or incidentally to some other use of this publication) without the written permission of the copyright owner, except in accordance with the provisions of the Copyright, Designs and Patents Act 1988 or under the terms of a licence issued by the Copyright Licensing Agency, Barnards Inn, 86 Fetter Lane, London EC4A 1EN (www.cla.co.uk). Applications for the copyright owner's written permission should be addressed to the publisher.

Printed in Slovakia by Neografia

Note from the publisher

Pearson has robust editorial processes, including answer and fact checks, to ensure the accuracy of the content in this publication, and every effort is made to ensure this publication is free of errors. We are, however, only human, and occasionally errors do occur. Pearson is not liable for any misunderstandings that arise as a result of errors in this publication, but it is our priority to ensure that the content is accurate. If you spot an error, please do contact us at resourcescorrections@pearson.com so we can make sure it is corrected.